HORROR,
FRIGHT,
and
PANIC

Recent Books by Margaret O. Hyde

Missing Children
Cancer in the Young: A Sense of Hope
Sexual Abuse: Let's Talk About It (revised edition)
Mind Drugs (fifth revised edition)
Cry Softly, the Story of Child Abuse (revised edition)
Know About Smoking
    and many others

Books by Elizabeth H. Forsyth
with Margaret O. Hyde

AIDS: What Does It Mean to You? (revised and expanded)
Terrorism: A Special Kind of Violence
Suicide: The Hidden Epidemic
What Have You Been Eating?
Know Your Feelings

HORROR, FRIGHT, and PANIC

**Margaret O. Hyde
and Elizabeth Forsyth, M.D.**

Revised and Expanded
from *Fears and Phobias*

Walker and Company

New York

First published in the United States of America
in 1987 by the Walker Publishing Company, Inc.

Published simultaneously in Canada by Thomas Allen & Son
Canada, Limited, Markham, Ontario

Library of Congress Cataloging-in-Publication Data

Hyde, Margaret O. (Margaret Oldroyd), 1917–
    Horror, fright, and panic.

    Rev. and expanded ed. of: Fears and phobias.
c1977.
    Includes index.
    1. Fear—Juvenile literature. 2. Horror—Juvenile
literature. 3. Panic—Juvenile literature.
I. Forsyth, Elizabeth Held. II. Hyde, Margaret O.
(Margaret Oldroyd), 1917–   Fears and phobias.
III. Title.
BF575.F2H93 1987   152.4   87-13312
ISBN 0-8027-6692-7
ISBN 0-8027-6693-5 (lib. bdg.)

Printed in the United States of America

10 9 8 7 6 5 4 3 2

To Eva and Martin Forsyth

Contents

Acknowledgments

The authors wish to thank the many professional associates and patients who contributed to this book. All names have been changed to preserve individual privacy. Special thanks go to Dr. David D. Burns for permission to use the Burns Anxiety Scale on pp. 68–69.

CHAPTER 1

The Age of Fear

Is this the Age of Fear? Fifty million Americans suffer from irrational fears or worries, and an additional 13 million have related disorders. Some experts consider anxiety disorders the most common mental-health problem today. Anxiety is the fifth most common medical or psychiatric diagnosis, and it accounted for 11 percent of all visits to medical doctors in a recent survey. In the past ten years, the medications most frequently prescribed in the United States have been anti-anxiety drugs such as Valium.

Consider the case of Cindy, a twenty-five-year-old woman who held a responsible job. Whenever she left home, she always felt nervous and shaky, and she became dizzy if she had to travel by bus or subway. The thought of crowds overwhelmed her, so she took a cab to work every day. She felt comfortable sitting at her desk and working, but she could not eat with her co-workers, because eating in public made her feel panicky. In order to avoid feeling anxious, she ate alone at her desk, even though she really would have preferred some companionship. Her anxieties kept her from making friends and prevented her from pursuing activities that she might have enjoyed. Cindy's fears controlled her life.

Anxiety itself is a universal human emotion that is as old as man. Early man may have feared thunder and lightning, while we fear nuclear disaster. The content changes, but the emotion is basically the same. Fear occurs in all mammals, and it serves a biological function.

Young monkeys and young children both have an inborn fear of separating from their mothers. This fear protects them from dangers in the environment while they are still too immature to protect themselves. Studies of monkey babies in the laboratory have shown that while they are young, the monkeys are very curious, and boldly investigate any new objects. At about one month of age, when they would normally start separating from their mothers in the forest, they react with fear to the same objects. Human babies demonstrate similar changes. Infants smile at everyone, but at about eight months of age, they begin to fear strange faces.

These observations suggest that separation fears protect the very young, and then as the child or animal matures and is apt to explore further afield, other fears take over the function of protection. These reactions to dangers have insured the survival of the species.

Family and twin studies seem to indicate that there may be an inherited tendency to anxiety reactions. One study of identical twins raised apart showed that the environment was not the determining factor. The researchers demonstrated that if one of a set of twins had an anxiety disorder, the other was found to have had a similar diagnosis. Anxiety states are more prevalent in females, but it is not clear whether heredity or learning accounts for the difference between the sexes.

Some fears appear to be widespread, and various studies have shown similar findings. In 1965, a random sampling of households in Burlington, Vermont, revealed that each person reported an average of seven fears. The most common were of snakes and small animals, heights, storms, flying, doctors, dentists, injury, illness, being alone, and enclosed spaces. The authors of this study concluded that there appeared to be three basic categories: fear of animals, fear of injury, and fear of separation.

Perhaps you cried at the age of two years when you lost your mother in the supermarket. You may have felt queasy and unsure on your first day in high school. Finding a mouse scurrying around in the kitchen makes your skin crawl. A car skids toward you as you cross an icy road, and you leap out of the way, heart pounding. Everyone has experienced these "normal" fears.

Suppose you are sitting in a quiet park late in the afternoon. The sunset casts a glow of orange light through the trees and all is peaceful. You are resting quietly when you hear something rustle, and a rat scurries across the walk to the trashcan. Suddenly there is a climate of fear. Your body reacts automatically and mobilizes its emergency system. Your heart rate increases, your hands feel cold, perspiration dampens your palms, and your mouth feels dry. Increased amounts of blood are sent to your brain and muscles. Your body is ready for "fight or flight," without any voluntary effort on your part. All these changes have occurred because the frightening cue, the rat, has mobilized your nervous system and sent messages to your endocrine glands, especially the pituitary and the adrenals. Your automatic reactions have prepared you for action, but the rat sneaks away, and once more you relax.

You are probably not the only one to experience fear in the park. Other animals respond to the environment with different senses and may experience varying amounts of fear because of your presence. The ant that crawls nearby lives in a very limited world and does not see you as it follows the track from its anthill to a source of food. The ant puts its nose to the ground, smelling its way with no fear that you might step on it and extinguish its existence. But if you crush some other ants, the first ant will exhibit some apparent signs of fear. No one really knows if the ant you have been watching is frightened by the crushed members of its own species, but it will appear to be frantic. This reaction may be due to the odor of the damaged ants. You, of course, will have no fear of the harmless little ant crawling through the grass beside you.

The frog croaking in the nearby pond doesn't see you either. Although the frog's field of vision is wide, it does not see very clearly. It is conscious only of fast-moving objects, such as the flies on which it feeds. But if you make a sudden move toward the frog, it will see a large body, assume you are an enemy, and be frightened enough to jump into the water to escape you. You probably will be amused rather than frightened.

Now suppose a snake is resting near the frog. What happens when it approaches the frog? The frog doesn't move. You might assume that the frog remains motionless because it is afraid of the snake, but that is not true. Actually, the frog does not move because it cannot see the small body slithering slowly in its direction. The frog's vision is limited to the kind it needs for catching insects.

What about the snake and you? The snake has an organ that is sensitive to heat and can warn the snake of danger when there is a temperature change of as little as $1/1,000$th of a degree centigrade. The snake may sense your presence by this detector and prepare to attack. At the same time, you are frightened by the snake because your eyes have detected it. But as the snake moves away from you, your sense of fear will gradually decrease.

A bird flies overhead. The bird does not frighten you, for it is no threat to your well-being and you actually enjoy watching it circle above, looking for food on the ground. The bird's vision is good, so good that it can watch a mouse from high in the sky. Suddenly, the bird swoops down to catch the mouse on the ground close to you, and for a moment you experience a pang of fear. But as the bird captures its prey and returns to the air, your fear disappears.

Bees fly near you as you rest on the bench. Even though they are small, you are mildly frightened because you know that they can sting you. But the bees do not see you as they fly straight ahead to gather nectar and pollen from the park flowers. Bees have eyes that see in a very special way. Their eyes are developed to see bright patterns of flowers in full bloom, the source of their nectar. Of course, if a bee happens to land on you and you injure it by brushing it or crushing part of it, the bee may sting in an effort to protect itself. People who are allergic to bee stings have good reason for the intense fear they experience when they hear the buzzing of a bee.

Plants that are familiar because of their poison may arouse fear in a person resting on the grass. If you roll over and discover you are lying in poison ivy, you may feel apprehensive because you know it can cause intense skin irritation. Nettles are another variety of plant that grows in meadows and causes pain to humans. A nettle bears a number of hairs and bristles that contain an irritating fluid. If you have walked or rolled in an area where these plants grow, you may be mildly frightened. The jagged splintery needles that are formed when the tip of a stinging nettle hair is broken penetrate human skin and leave a sting that may last only half an hour, but may cause severe burning and itching during that time. Although one does not usually panic at the sight of nettle plants, anyone familiar with them may feel a few pangs of fear when falling in their direction.

When the sky grows dark, certain noises may frighten you. Nighthawks climb high in the sky above you, beating their long wings. As they come back toward earth, their eerie cries pierce the air at regular intervals.

More frightening to most people is the sight of a bat, which may dart from a tree or a chimney and sweep toward the grass in search of gnats and moths. Many people have heard that bats can steer away from obstacles (such as people) in their paths, but you may still find bats frightening. If such is the case, the climate of fear is confined to your own body, for the bat is unaware of your presence. It is sending out signals somewhat like the clicking noise that you can make with your tongue, but you do not hear the signals because they are so high-pitched that no human can hear them. This special radar system helps the bat locate its prey. Adjusting its position to that of the insect it has detected, the bat snaps up the insect and continues its search for food. After the bat flies away, your body quickly readjusts to a situation of peaceful rest.

Consider the things that might trigger your fear in a park, in a field, or in any other place, for that matter. In every case, they are creatures, plants, objects, or experiences that have some potential to harm you or that you think will harm you. One definition of fear is *a reaction to a recognized threat that is characterized by an impulse to escape danger and a feeling of disagreeable tension.*

The intensity of fear in any situation varies among individuals and depends partly on the potential danger that causes the fear. While fears in the field, in the city, or in any other place might range from very mild fright to panic, there is no exact way to measure them except in the laboratory. But it is clear that to some degree humans, dogs, cats, and many other animals all experience the natural reactions of fight or flight in various stressful situations.

Now suppose you are sitting in the same grassy field, feeling relaxed, but there are no snakes or other animals to disturb the peace. Suddenly, you experience fear, a feeling that something dreadful is going to happen. Your heart is thumping and skips a beat. You tremble and feel faint. These are the same feelings experienced in response to a real fear, but in this case, there is no immediate threat.

This is anxiety, and it differs from fear in that anxiety has no readily discernible cause, or the emotion may be out of proportion to the cause. It might be said that this abnormal fear response represents a protective mechanism gone awry.

Anxiety can be mild and occasional, such as the kind you might experience during an encounter with a snake in a meadow or during a bumpy plane flight. Or it may be generalized, non-specific, and persistent, occurring over a period of time, with constant feelings of tension, jitteriness, apprehension, irritability, worry, and various physical symptoms such as palpitations, increased pulse rate, cold, clammy hands, and upset stomach.

Some people have recurrent attacks of intense anxiety that strike suddenly and that seem to have no cause. These are panic attacks. They can be truly terrifying, and their physical and mental manifestations can feel worse than any other kind of pain.

It is not uncommon for people to have irrational fears of specific situations or things that they can usually manage to avoid. For instance, if you had a mild fear of snakes, you might not want to sit in a meadow, and you might not visit the snake house at the zoo. In other words, your slight fear of snakes would not restrict your life. Suppose, however, that you became so fearful and apprehensive at the thought of encountering a snake that you could not even walk down a country road or go anywhere near a zoo. This reaction would qualify as a phobia, since it causes considerable anxiety and interferes with your life.

Severe forms of anxiety can be extremely disabling and distressing. Sufferers are often misunderstood by their families, friends, and even their physicians. Because anxiety is a universal experience, other people may underestimate the seriousness of the symptoms and may become impatient with the affected person. They might think that a vacation, a rest, a joint, or a few drinks will cure the condition. Someone who has panic attacks may be convinced that he or she is suffering from a physical ailment because of the many physical symptoms that accompany these attacks. The person often goes from one doctor to another, trying to find a cause for the frightening and puzzling symptoms.

A host of medical conditions may cause anxiety-like symptoms. Low blood sugar, thyroid disease, certain tumors that secrete hormones, and chronic lung disease are just a few of them. Anxiety occurs in numerous mental disorders, as well. Depressed people often suffer from anxiety. Drugs like cocaine and marijuana, alcohol, and even excessive coffee-drinking can cause anxiety.

Other circumstances, such as stressful life events and early childhood experiences, can trigger anxiety. Sigmund Freud, the father of psychoanalysis, thought that phobias were caused by unconscious or buried conflicts. Although not all psychiatrists agree with Freudian psychoanalytic theories, these theories do not necessarily exclude the notion that there is some biological basis for anxiety disorders. Freud himself thought that there was a biological predisposition for many psychological problems.

Some experts, like Dr. Aaron Beck, a psychiatrist at the University of Pennsylvania, point out that there is a relationship between anxiety disorders and the way people interpret their experiences; anxious people have distorted perceptions and self-defeating habits. For instance, Jennifer gets a tremendous thrill from riding a roller coaster in the amusement park. Susan might experience the same physical sensations in her stomach as Jennifer while plummeting down, but she interprets them as a signal that she is having a heart attack and feels very apprehensive and uncomfortable. Situations that some find anxiety-provoking are considered challenges by others.

Some people think they must always be perfect. They feel that if they are not always in perfect control they are showing weakness. This kind of individual may become anxious when faced with uncertainties or with the thought of losing control.

No single theory explains everything. Researchers have accumulated a large body of knowledge about anxiety disorders, and most agree that there are multiple factors: genetic, biological, and psychological. Biology can influence behavior, but behavior also affects biological processes.

CHAPTER 2

Panic

Suppose you are rushing down the street to the library. You have had a busy day, you are tired, but you must pick up the books you need for your term paper. As you run up the steps, you begin to feel woozy, your heart starts thumping and skips a beat, and there is a tightness in your chest. You sit down at the nearest table, unable to control your rapid breathing. Your face feels numb, your mouth is dry, and you see black spots, and you think you may be about to faint. Everything seems unreal and peculiar. When you try to concentrate on remembering which books you wanted, you can only think about how awful you feel. Somehow, you manage to find the books and check them out. You are afraid that something terrible is going to happen, and that you may lose control. You are desperate to get home. When you arrive at last, you lie down; the uneasy feeling is still there, and your heart is still beating uncomfortably fast, but finally you relax and fall asleep.

The next day, you feel fine. But what caused those symptoms? You might have thought you were going crazy, coming down with influenza, or even having a heart attack. You go to your physician for a check-up, just to reassure yourself, and she finds no physical or mental problems.

The following week, you go back to the library. As you are looking through the card catalogue, you suddenly feel uneasy and uncomfortable again, and your vision dims. Your heart is pounding, and you feel as though you are suffocating. You grab your coat and race out of the library. The attack subsides quickly as you sit quietly on the front steps, but you are worried because now you are sure that you have a serious illness. What you actually may have experienced is a panic attack.

It is said that the ancient Greek god, Pan, amused himself by frightening mortals who ventured into the lonely woods where he lived. The word "panic" is derived from the contagious fear he caused. Common examples of situations causing panic reactions are fires, explosions, and earthquakes. For instance, a fire breaks out in a theater, and people have begun walking out in an orderly fashion. Suddenly a few individuals start to push their way through the group. The whole crowd stampedes in panic toward the exits, clogging them so that no one escapes. Most people think of panic as an irrational, unthinking response to a catastrophe. In fact, however, panic as a reaction to catastrophe is rare. Panic is more likely to occur as an episode of overwhelming anxiety with no apparent cause, which attacks people without warning, just as it attacked the student in the library.

Anxiety and fear are normal emotions. Fear is a rational response to immediate danger, usually external, while anxiety generally lacks a clear or easily definable cause. Anxiety may be described as worry, tension, apprehension, or uneasiness. Everyone has experienced anxiety in stressful situations of everyday life—taking final exams, playing the piano in a recital, preparing for a college or job interview. This kind of anxiety is normal, short-lived, and generally does not cause any significant difficulties. It may actually improve your performance because it stimulates you to cope with problems, heightens your alertness, and motivates achievement. But when anxiety becomes persistent, severe, and irrational, it can be disabling, interfering with a person's life and his or her ability to function.

A panic attack, with its sudden onset of intense fear and

feelings of impending doom, accompanied by the various physical sensations described earlier, is extremely distressing to the sufferer. Until recently, this disorder was not fully recognized. In the past, anxiety states have been described by various labels— soldier's heart, hysterical vertigo, cardiac neurosis, irritable heart, and neurocirculatory asthenia. There are many historical descriptions of anxiety attacks. In the seventeenth century, churchman Robert Burton wrote in *The Anatomy of Melancholy,* ". . . this fear causeth in man, as to be red, pale, tremble, sweat; it makes sudden cold and heat to come over all the body . . . Many men are so amazed and astonished with fear they know not where they are, what they say, what they do. . . ." Anyone who has suffered from stage fright can testify to the accuracy of this description.

The search for causes of anxiety produced an interesting assortment of unfounded theories over the years, ranging from "fermentation dyspepsia," masturbation, and small heart to low blood chlorides and low blood sugar. Most of these old theories have no basis in fact.

The physical symptoms are so marked that even in the 1960's, attacks were sometimes regarded as fainting spells. On occasion, panic attacks are mistaken for heart disease, and people are admitted to coronary-care units. After repeated medical examinations by doctors not familiar with the disorder, some sufferers have made the correct diagnosis themselves, upon learning about it from television or in magazines. One author noted that all the patients he interviewed had had prior medical consultations, and 70 percent of them had consulted more than ten doctors.

Many people who experience a panic attack think that it is bizarre or crazy and do not realize that they are not unique. One study done in 1985 suggested that as many as 3 percent of the adult population had some kind of panic attack during a six-month period. Other estimates range as high as 3 to 5 percent of women and .8 percent of men. This means that perhaps 15 million people have experienced panic attacks. The first attack usually occurs before age twenty-five, between the ages of fifteen and twenty, according to some researchers, and it generally happens in a public place.

If you were the young person who had experienced two panic attacks in the library, how would you feel? You would probably worry about when the next attack might occur.

Two days later, you return to the library, but this time, when you come within half a block, you begin to feel anxious and uneasy, and you remember how uncomfortable you felt the last time you were here. You walk more slowly, feeling more and more apprehensive. Finally, you decide to go home and finish writing up your physics laboratory report instead. This decision relieves your tension. But what about the next time? You are a student and you cannot avoid the library.

Something new has happened: in addition to the panic attacks, you are becoming anxious when you think about the necessity of going to the library. The anxiety has spread. This is a typical story. At first, the person may feel mildly uncomfortable and then begin to avoid the places where an attack might occur. Gradually, he or she may even become anxious at the thought of leaving the safety of home, because a panic attack could occur anywhere. Some individuals may become so anxiety-ridden that they slowly curtail their freedom and literally become prisoners in their own homes. They give up all their activities because of the fear that they may provoke a panic attack. Many people feel safe only if someone accompanies them when they go out. Not surprisingly, these individuals become isolated from others and often experience depression.

This fear of going out is known as agoraphobia, literally, fear of the marketplace. A phobia may be defined as an intense, illogical, irrational, abnormal fear of a specific thing or situation. The fear in agoraphobia is not really directly related to being out in public, but rather it is anxiety about losing control in public, and worrying about what might happen. It has been called the fear of fear. Although someone may develop agoraphobia without having experienced panic attacks, in many cases agoraphobia is preceded by panic attacks. There is some controversy among researchers as to the relationship between agoraphobia and panic attacks. Some experts think that a panic attack is just another form of anxiety, but most think it is fundamentally different.

Jeff is a young man who sought medical help because he feels dizzy and unsteady on his feet. Neurologists and other specialists have found nothing wrong with him. He refuses to leave his house except to go to work, but at home and at work, he spends all his time in a recliner chair, which is the only place he feels comfortable. If he has to walk, he leans on the walls. Jeff is an only child whose mother was very nervous and overprotective. He always became very fearful when his parents went out or left him for any reason, and he worried that they might die, or that he might die. He never slept over at a friend's house and never went to summer camp. At age seven, he developed a school phobia, which is really a fear of leaving home, not a fear of going to school. His panic attacks, with symptoms of dizziness, began shortly after he broke up with his girlfriend at age twenty-four.

Researchers have found that 20 to 50 percent of people who suffer from panic attacks were overly attached to their families as children, and that many had school phobias when they were young. As in Jeff's case, there is often a loss or separation, such as the death of someone close, or the breakup of a marriage, which precedes the first attack.

Much of the most recent investigation into the causes of the panic syndrome points to a biological predisposition. Panic attacks may be part of a biological disorder that involves the central nervous system. Dr. Peter J. Hauri, professor of psychiatry at

Dartmouth and director of the Sleep Disorders Clinic, compared the sleep patterns of normal sleepers and insomniacs with those of people who suffered from panic disorder. He found that during non-dreaming sleep, the panic patients showed signs such as eye movements, facial twitching, and rapid heart rate. Half the patients actually awakened with full-blown panic attacks. The fact that panic occurs when the mind is "shut off," i.e., not experiencing dream anxiety, suggests a biological cause for this disorder.

Other studies have demonstrated that people with panic disorders are more sensitive than others to substances such as caffeine, marijuana, carbon dioxide, and sodium lactate. Lactic acid, a chemical in the blood, is a product of metabolism, which increases during exercise. Various researchers have found that individuals with panic attacks are more prone to attacks during physical exertion, and they produce excessive amounts of lactic acid compared with normal controls. Furthermore, in laboratory studies, when sodium lactate solution is injected into the bloodstream of volunteers, 50 to 70 percent of the panic-prone individuals suffer attacks, compared with only 10 percent of the controls. Research suggests that some people may have an underlying imbalance of certain substances called neurotransmitters, which are active in the nervous system.

Recently, many researchers have become interested in an abnormality known as mitral valve prolapse, or MVP. The mitral valve is a valve between two of the heart's chambers, the left atrium and the left ventricle. In this disorder, the valve billows back into the atrium and causes a murmur. Although many people with this condition do not have any symptoms, others have palpitations, chest pain or discomfort, breathlessness, fatigue, or anxiety. In the past, MVP may have been responsible for the disorder known as "neurocirculatory asthenia" or "soldier's heart." Some physicians thought the condition was due to heart disease, while others considered it a cardiac neurosis. With the technology available today, physicians can diagnose MVP accurately by using echocardiography, which permits them to visualize the inside of the heart without actually invading the body. MVP occurs in about 10 percent of the general population, and in most cases, does not mean actual heart disease, but may be a harmless disorder of function. There is a connection between MVP and panic disorder, but the relationship is not clear. Investigators have found that between 30 and 50 percent of people with panic attacks have mitral valve prolapse. Some researchers have suggested that there is an underlying, inborn vulnerability of the nervous system that might cause the predisposition to panic disorder as well as MVP in some people. Another theory is that MVP may be one of a number of activating factors that can contribute to the development of panic disorder.

While there is a large body of evidence supporting the existence of some biological and inherited predisposition to panic attacks, it is important to realize that psychological factors and learning can play a large part as well. As one writer points out, the medical approach ignores *what* a person is anxious about.

CHAPTER 3

The Many Faces of Fear

If you suffered from mysophobia, nyctophobia, potamophobia, or topophobia, what would you be worried about? (The answer: fear of dirt, germs, or contamination; fear of the dark; fear of running water; or stage fright.) These impressive names with Greek roots are labels for just a few of the so-called simple phobias.

The following is a list of names of other phobias for those who enjoy collecting unusual words.

Acrophobia	heights
Agoraphobia	open spaces, the marketplace
Ailurophobia	cats
Anthropophobia	people
Arachnophobia	spiders
Astrophobia	lightning
Brontophobia	thunder
Claustrophobia	enclosed spaces
Cynophobia	dogs
Equinophobia	horses
Herpetophobia	reptiles
Murophobia	mice

Pyrophobia	fire
Thanatophobia	death
Xenophobia	strangers
Zoophobia	animals

A simple phobia is fear of a specific object, situation, or activity, and it differs from a common fear mainly in degree. Most everyday fears cause little discomfort or interference with one's normal life, but a phobia may be severely limiting. There are hundreds of things and situations that people fear. Maybe you are afraid of bees and heights, and you get very nervous when you go to the dentist. But your fears do not really qualify as phobias unless they interfere with your functioning in school, work, social relationships, or other activities.

Dr. Stewart Agras, professor of psychiatry at Stanford University and expert in the field of anxiety disorders, cites the example of a woman who had a frog phobia. Most people would not be bothered by such a minor fear. How many frogs does one encounter every day when taking the subway to school? But Dr. Agras's patient lived in rural Vermont, where many frogs also live during the spring and summer. She had given up her career because she could not leave her house for fear of encountering frogs.

In addition to the fear itself, phobics suffer from anticipatory anxiety, that is, worry about the possibility of confronting the feared situation. They avoid anxiety by keeping away from the object or situation that they fear, as in the case of the woman who stayed in her house to avoid frogs. When these individuals are confronted with the phobic situation, their reaction may be very intense, like the panic reaction described in the previous chapter. The difference is that phobics do not experience spontaneous panic attacks. They become anxious only in relation to a specific fear. Most phobics know that their fears are not sensible, and that there is nothing to be afraid of, but that knowledge does not help.

Sometimes people with phobias develop rituals to help them avoid anxiety. Joanne, a young woman who had a germ phobia, washed her hands many times a day. Her fear of germs progressed so that she felt it was necessary to wash even the clean dishes before she used them. She was unable to eat until she had performed all the compulsive rituals that she thought would prevent her from becoming contaminated by germs. She washed all the dishes first, then she scrubbed the table and counters and scoured the sink with bleach. Before she prepared the food, she scalded it with hot water. Joanne had to carry out her elaborate precautions in a certain way in order to feel safe from the feared germs and to avoid becoming anxious. Even though she knew these rituals were becoming excessive and extremely time-consuming, she could not make herself stop, because the rituals calmed her anxieties.

Literature and history abound with descriptions of irrational fears. Many centuries ago, the Greek physician Hippocrates recounted the story of a man who became terrified when he heard the sound of a flute, but only at night, and only when he was drinking. It is said that King James I of England experienced fear whenever he saw an unsheathed sword.

Early writers thought that fears might be transmitted from the mother to her unborn child during pregnancy. According to this theory, King James was afraid of swords because his mother had witnessed the murder of a friend while pregnant with James. Although there are still some people who believe that fears or other attributes can be acquired in such a manner, this is not the case.

At the beginning of the twentieth century, Freud published his famous case history of a phobic boy, known as "Little Hans." This is a classic example of phobia, which is often cited. Hans was a five-year-old boy who developed a fear of going out in the street because he was terrified that a horse might bite him. These symptoms began after Hans had seen an accident involving a horse-drawn bus. Freud saw Hans only once and carried on the analysis mainly through correspondence with the boy's father. Freud concluded that the phobia was rooted in unresolved, unconscious sexual conflicts. He theorized that little Hans wanted his mother all to himself and was afraid that his father would retaliate. He therefore unconsciously replaced his fear of the father's retribution with the fear of being bitten by a horse. In this way, he could avoid horses, and thus avoid the anxiety. According to Freud, phobias stem from the unconscious conflict between the desire to gratify sexual or aggressive impulses and the recognition that danger might result from satisfying these wishes. The phobia represents this unconscious conflict. Not everyone agrees with this theory. In the case of Hans, there could be a number of interpretations, but no one can be sure which one is correct, especially since the analysis was carried on through Hans's father. Some psychiatrists think that it was simply seeing the accident that caused Hans to develop the phobia.

Another classic study was the case of "Little Albert," published by the psychologist John B. Watson in 1920. Watson and his colleagues wanted to demonstrate that a fear could be produced experimentally, so they performed an experiment that would be considered cruel and unethical today. Albert was an eleven-month-old baby and the son of a wet nurse in a home for invalid children, who was reared from birth in this hospital environment. He was a husky child who rarely cried or showed any fear. When presented with animals such as a white rat, a rabbit, a monkey, and a dog, as well as objects like masks and burning newspapers, he was not frightened, but reached out to touch them. He cried only when a loud noise was made. For the experiment, the white rat was presented to Albert. When he reached for it, a loud noise was made by striking a steel bar behind Albert's head. This startled him, and he began to cry. After the fifth repetition of this pairing of the rat with the noise,

Albert reacted with crying as soon as he saw the rat. Later, the fear was generalized to other furry objects such as a rabbit, a Santa Claus mask, a fur neckpiece, and fluffy material.

Watson succeeded in inducing a phobia by the method of conditioning. This suggested another hypothesis to explain the development of phobias in life outside the laboratory. However, this theory, known as learning theory, leaves some questions unanswered. For instance, most cases of phobia do not appear to have started with a traumatic incident, although some do. Some people who were sexually abused as children may grow up with fears and anxieties about sex.

Occasionally the phobic individual has forgotten the incident, which later may be uncovered during the course of psychotherapy. One woman whom Dr. Agras treated was so claustrophobic that she had had the door and all the windows removed from her bedroom, for the fresh air she thought she needed in order to sleep, even though she lived in an extremely cold part of the country. She recalled a day in her childhood when she was playing with her friends in a shop that belonged to the father of one of the children. He was an undertaker, and the shop had several empty coffins. When she climbed into one of the coffins on a dare, her friends closed the lid and would not let her out. After that terrifying experience, she became claustrophobic.

Learning theory as an explanation for phobias does not explain why fears conditioned by association in the laboratory are generally short-lived, while in real life, phobias are usually very persistent. One explanation may lie in the finding from laboratory experiments with rats, for example, that avoiding the feared object blocks the normal process of unlearning the phobic response. Most phobic individuals manage to stay away from the situations or objects that produce anxiety, and therefore the irrational fear persists.

For example, take the case of Eric. He was afraid that he

might choke if his throat became too dry, so he carried a water bottle with him everywhere, even though he very rarely needed to take a drink from it. However, when he was prevented from taking the bottle, he became very anxious, and he experienced the physical symptoms of anxiety, among which was dry mouth. This, of course, made him even more fearful of choking and made his mouth even drier. It was a vicious cycle, and it reinforced his fear more strongly.

Some researchers have suggested the idea of "evolutionarily prepared learning." This refers to the observation that certain responses are more easily learned than others, and that there may be some inborn preparedness that makes some things more readily feared than others. In 1929, the English psychologist C. S. Valentine recorded the following study performed on his own small daughter. While the child was sitting on her mother's lap, she reached for a pair of opera glasses on a nearby table. Valentine blew a shrill blast on a whistle each time she reached for the glasses. Although she turned to see what the noise was, she did not cry. Later in the day, her brother brought her a woolly caterpillar. She had never before been so close to a caterpillar, so it was strange to her. She turned away, then turned back, and as she did so, there was a blast on the whistle. This time she screamed in fright.

Valentine reported that he repeated the process four times and that his daughter screamed in terror each time. He thought that the whistle accentuated her attitude toward the caterpillar. The noise produced the slight added stimulus to make her fear of the woolly creature burst forth. This experiment seemed to indicate that there was something special about the caterpillar that was not present with the opera glasses.

Like Watson, Valentine seemed to have been so interested in his experiment that he disregarded the child's terror. Psychologists today would be more sensitive to the child's feelings.

More recent experiments in the laboratory, using sophisticated instruments to record physiological changes in human volunteers, have borne out this theory. Mild electric shocks are used, and the electrical resistance of the skin is recorded, as the resistance changes with anxiety. These studies show that it is easier to link a response of fear with snakes or spiders than with flowers or abstract shapes. In other studies, researchers have been able to induce a "mini-phobia" to a picture of an angry face, but not to a smiling face. It has been noted again and again that people tend to fear insects, snakes, and certain other animals. Perhaps humans are born with a built-in readiness to acquire fears to certain potentially dangerous situations, like animals, darkness, and heights.

Numerous observations of primates have produced evidence that fear can be learned in another way. In one experiment, young monkeys were used who had no fear of snakes, since they were raised in the laboratory. These monkeys were allowed to observe their parents reacting fearfully to the presence of both real and toy snakes. It took only eight minutes for the young ones to develop a marked fear of the snakes. It was also noted that the more disturbed the parents had acted, the more fearful the young monkeys became. The monkeys transmitted their fear through interaction with each other.

Human parents, too, can transmit fears to their offspring. Learning in the family situation plays a very important part in the way children develop. As noted earlier, school phobia is not really a phobia, but separation anxiety. People who are prone to phobic anxiety as adults often have a history of school phobia as children. Many parents communicate fear to their children, both verbally and non-verbally, by acting overprotective. One mother who was leaving her son at nursery school for the first time said goodbye several times, kept reassuring him that she was really coming back to pick him up at noon, and then told him not to cry. The little boy finally burst into tears and begged her not to leave. Although not especially anxious at first, he learned from his mother that separating from her might be scary.

Although there is still much to discover about the development of the anxiety disorders, panic, and phobias, investigators have enough knowledge to help people overcome these distressing conditions.

CHAPTER 4

Children's Fears

The fears of very young children come and go. One day two-year-old David will scream when he hears the noise of a vacuum cleaner. He is terrified now, but yesterday he paid no attention to it. He heard no other loud noises yesterday or today that might have caused this new fear. But David's fear of this noise is a common one at age two, and will probably disappear as suddenly as it arose.

Certain fears are quite common in young children, and they appear at various ages as a child learns and matures. What is normal at one time may be considered abnormal at another age. Five-year-old Ted was afraid of the neighbor's large dog, a common fear at his age. At age twelve, he was still avoiding all dogs, because they made him feel anxious, even though no dog had ever attacked him. At this age, Ted's fear is considered abnormal. It is common for preschoolers to be fearful of animals, strangers, and the dark. As young children acquire more knowledge and skills, and as they begin to conquer the unknown, they become more confident and the early fears disappear. New fears appear at about age twelve or thirteen. Fears of dying sometimes develop at this stage, because until this point, children do not really appreciate the full meaning of death.

Can you remember some of the things that frightened you when you were very young? Most of the things that frighten young children are quickly forgotten, but this is not always the case.

One woman named Lucy was unable to discard a childhood fear of automobiles. She consulted a therapist, Dr. Charles Odier, who described her case in his book, *Patterns of Magical Thinking.* It was through a dream that Lucy recalled the origin of her fear. She dreamed that a baby in a carriage was run over by a large automobile. She recognized herself as the baby in the dream. After this, Lucy was able to recall a terrifying experience from her early childhood in which she was paralyzed by fear while playing in the garden near the garage. As a child, she had imagined the garage to be a big cage. When a car came out of it, she associated the noise of the motor with the loud roar of an animal coming to get her. Although in later years she forgot the experience, she continued to suffer from intense fear of cars. Her fear of automobiles occurred only when she was outside a car. Then she would automatically say, "Here comes a crusher!" To her, all drivers were "crushers" who were out to kill pedestrians. Her case was very complex, but what is of interest here is the fact that Lucy's phobia had its roots in her childhood when she imagined the car to be an animal that was intent on harming her. Her acute feeling of helplessness as a young child grew into such anxiety that all cars appeared dangerous to her unless she was riding safely within. Like the claustrophobic woman described in an earlier chapter, who had been shut in a coffin as a child, Lucy developed a phobia. But relatively few children experience fears that are so traumatic that they develop into phobias. In addition, the origins of most phobias cannot be traced to specific traumatic events, as noted earlier.

Every healthy child experiences fears. Newborns react to intense, unexpected noises. This reaction, called the startle response, is present at birth and is inborn. Although fear is difficult to examine in the very young because it is not possible to interpret an infant's expressions with certainty, some studies have yielded interesting results. The fear of an approaching object appears to be present early in life. Some infants as young as two weeks showed apparent fear reactions in an experiment done with over forty babies. A small rubber cube was moved to within eight inches of a baby's face. Each time this was done, the infant cried loudly, put its hands between its face and the object, and pulled away from it.

Great Aunt Tillie might be less upset by baby's shrieks when she moves close to express love if she realized that babies are instinctively frightened by the approach of a stranger.

Fear of strangers appears to be almost universal in infants in the second half of the first year of life. While 98 percent of a sample group of infants between the ages of two and six months will smile in response to the face of any individual, indiscriminate smiling usually ceases after that age. Dr. Marshall Klaus of Case Western Reserve University in Cleveland, Ohio, has studied the facial bonding between mother and child, which he believed occurs during the first few hours of life. This is the first evidence of social interaction in humans and is believed to form the basis for further social learning.

Once babies can distinguish faces at about six months, they react to strangers with fear. This fear usually continues until the first birthday and sometimes through the second year of life. The fear response is a further stage in social interaction.

The fear behavior of one-year-olds usually varies according to the nearness of the mother or father. For example, in one experiment there was less evidence of fear in a stressful situation when a baby was in the mother's lap than when the mother moved four feet away from the child. Another factor that influences the fear reaction at this age is the stranger's behavior. When the baby was not touched and the stranger smiled and played peek-a-boo, there were some positive reactions from one-year-olds.

Fear of strangers is considered just one aspect of the fear of new situations or things. Studies of thousands of normal children have shown that many fears do come and go in a somewhat ordered pattern. Although each child exhibits some individual variations, most two-year-olds are afraid of loud noises, and few children seem to fear the dark before the age of two or three. At two and a half, children generally fear moving objects, such as large trucks, and people who appear unexpectedly from a place such as a door not commonly used.

Fear of animals is common to most children and seems to begin at the age of three. Five-year-olds are less afraid of animals in general, but they are more apprehensive of being bitten by a dog. They are also afraid of bodily harm, of falling, and of mother's not returning when she goes out at night.

Fear of the dark continues for a number of years but usually lessens by the time a child is eight or nine. Fear of ghosts and witches, haunted houses, or other supernatural phenomena continues for several years. Of course, some people never outgrow these and other fears. A great many young children who read about lions, tigers, and dinosaurs, as well as the supernatural, seek reassurance from their parents that these fierce beasts are not in the backyard or immediate environment. One of the major sources of trust in authority comes from the relief from anxiety that a young child experiences on being told that there are *no* lions and *no* dinosaurs anywhere nearby.

While ten-year-olds are not especially fearful, wild animals and snakes are commonly feared at this age. As the child's horizons broaden, fears that are not so personal are introduced. Television, books, and radio may stimulate other fears.

While each age has its characteristic fears, most pass harmlessly. It helps when people realize that fear is not shameful and that it is natural for a child to withdraw from those things that seem harmful. This is typical of survival patterns in young and old and in other animals as well as humans. For example, fear of heights is common to many animals as well as to the very young child.

Psychologist Eleanor Gibson was picnicking one day on the rim of the Grand Canyon when she wondered whether or not a young baby would recognize the danger at the brink or would fall off into space. Her speculations led to some famous experiments that are known as the visual cliff experiments. An arrangement of simulated levels was used. The effect of a one-foot drop was created by placing a piece of heavy glass some 12 inches above a piece of patterned material. A board at the same level as the glass was covered with the same patterned material. On the side opposite the simulated drop, or "cliff" side, was another sheet of glass with the patterned material immediately beneath it, giving the appearance of a shallow drop.

For the experiments, young children were placed on the board while their mothers called from the cliff side. In general, children peered down at the glass and backed away from what looked like the steep side—even after they'd touched the glass. Babies as young as six months discerned that the patterned material seemed far beneath them and were afraid of falling off. Of thirty-six infants tested over a period of time, only three crept off the "brink" onto the glass suspended a foot above the pattern.

Chickens less than 24 hours old were tested on the visual cliff, and they, too, avoided the deep area. Young goats and lambs were tested as soon as they could stand, and no goat or lamb ever stepped off the deep side. Kittens "froze" or crawled backward when placed on the glass over the deep side.

From these and numerous other experiments, it seems clear that in many species of animals fear or perception of height appears very early. Even infants who have never experienced the sensation of falling seem to fear falling off a cliff.

Loss of support and sudden loud noises also cause fear

The visual cliff. Redrawn from *Sight and Mind* by Lloyd Kaufman,
Oxford University Press, 1974.

responses in most young infants, as well as in animals of other
species. Despite this and other common fear responses, however, experimenters such as Alexander Thomas, Stella Chess,
and Herbert G. Birch report that children do show distinct
individuality in temperament in the first weeks of life. This
difference is independent of the treatment they receive and of
their parents' personalities. Thomas et al. studied the response of
an infant to a new object or person in order to see whether the
child would accept the new experience or withdraw from it. In
most cases, a child's original reaction seemed to be retained over
the years, although temperaments can and do change.

Consider the case of Grace. From the start, she probably
cried loudly when someone slammed a door in the hospital
nursery even though other babies continued to sleep. Through-
out infancy Grace had withdrawal reactions whenever she faced
a new situation, such as entering kindergarten, or encountered a
new challenge. But these withdrawal reactions were soon forgotten because Grace always adjusted well once the newness wore
off. Grace had many friends and few problems until the fifth
grade, when she had to transfer to a new and larger school. The
move caused her great fear and worry. These emotions puzzled
her parents until her history was reviewed and it was recognized
that she had a fundamental tendency to withdraw from new

situations and to adapt to them slowly. Understanding of a person's temperament can help in dealing with a wide variety of situations.

Sometimes, anxious children do not outgrow their fears and continue to be fearful. They may worry about everything in their lives, like grades in school, whether their classmates like them, or about bad things that might happen. They may be scared of the dark or of being alone. They are often overly sensitive and shy and may avoid other children because they feel awkward and uncomfortable. If overly anxious children do not receive help in overcoming their fears, they may grow up to be withdrawn and worried adults who cannot enjoy life fully.

Fear of darkness is one of the possibly preprogrammed fears that sometimes continues long after childhood. Children are commonly afraid of the dark, perhaps because two natural cues are present when one is alone in the dark: strangeness and isolation. An inky black room is a totally unfamiliar place. Things that are familiar in daylight often take on strange forms at night. A dimly lit basement has shadowy recesses. Bedroom curtains that blow in the wind form strange shadows. There is also a fear of being attacked when one is in the dark, so it is not surprising that this fear is so common.

Most parents attempt to help their children overcome the fear of the dark in many ways. Some parents, however, are unusually cruel and use the child's fear to obtain good or desired behavior. A parent may threaten to lock a child in a dark room or closet if s/he does not behave, and for some children, this threat becomes a reality. Fortunately, most parents help their children overcome the fear of the dark by reassuring them that they are nearby, thus eliminating one natural cue (that of being alone) and making the darkness far less frightening.

Three psychologists, Frederick H. Kanfer, Paul Karoly, and Alexander Newman, experimented with forty-five kindergarten children in a large midwestern city in the United States. They wanted to find out if they could reduce fear of darkness more effectively through the popular psychological technique known as systematic desensitization if they combined it with verbal cues. The children were chosen carefully. All were so afraid of the dark that they would not remain alone in a dark room for more than a very brief time. The average time at the beginning of the experiment was 27 seconds.

The experiment was carried out in a darkened schoolroom, which was familiar to the children. It was conducted in a scientific manner, with some children acting as a control group (one that was given neutral information). Each child was in contact with an experimenter by electronic equipment, and each could illuminate the room at will. The experimental group was divided in two. One, known as the competence group, used the verbal clue: "I am a brave boy. I can take care of myself in the dark." The other, called the stimulus group, was taught to verbalize as follows: "The dark is a fun place to be. There are many good things in the dark." The control group used "Mary had a little lamb. Its fleece was white as snow."

The experimenters were careful not to frighten the children, and they worked with a complicated procedure. They obtained the best results with children in the competence group and observed that stressing the child's competence to deal with the dark resulted in the longest tolerance times. The neutral and stimulus groups did not differ from each other in ability to stay alone in the dark.

While this experiment was complex and involved many more factors than can be explained here, it does illustrate one way in which fear of darkness can be handled. Just the simple assurance that parents, or someone they know, will come when called is enough to make the dark less frightening for many children. And this fear, as with many other fears of children, does tend to disappear. However, even adults who suffer from a fear of the darkness can be sure that their fear is shared by a large number of people. From childhood days to old age, many people suffer at the very thought of speaking in front of a group even though they may be well qualified to do so. Standing up alone makes them feel uncomfortable, while speaking as part of a group is less apt to cause fear. Perhaps this is related to the fear of isolation and the desire to be close to an attachment figure. Consider a three-year-old girl who is frightened by the dark and clutches her teddy bear. Two children walk past a haunted house holding hands. Two adults are frightened by a noise while camping out, so they move their sleeping bags closer together. An earthquake causes damage in a village, and the people draw closer together both physically and emotionally.

Although most people reach out to their friends and relatives in time of danger, there are people who are afraid to make friends. The attachment to mother is normally formed without conscious effort, and for most people, both young and old, the same is true in forming friendships. But there are many people who are so conscious of their supposed shortcomings that they are afraid to risk rejection by their peers. This is especially true during adolescence, but it carries over into the lives of some adults.

Fear of not being accepted is a common fear that allows peer groups to set such standards as the "right thing to wear" and the "right thing to say and do." As young people or children grow away from parents and reach out toward the larger world, fears of not being popular, of not having the money to keep up with the group, of being laughed at, of not being liked by the opposite sex, and of being lonely are very common, private fears. A lonely person feels frighteningly unarmed and unprotected.

Those who experience the fear of love, even though they do not recognize this fear, are the people who feel alone in a crowd. They may not even be able to relate comfortably to their own immediate families. Some people have a fear of experiencing good feelings, and this may be related to a fear that they are not lovable.

The fact that loneliness is a form of separation seems obvious, but the degree to which most people fear separation is not. Life begins with separation at birth, and it is here that some professionals believe chronic fear, or anxiety, begins. A baby enters a world that is very different from the secure one it has known in the mother's uterus. Otto Rank, a leading psychoanalyst, presented the theory that birth is such a frightening experience that a person never completely outgrows the fears it creates. Other authorities say that birth is the first experience to activate the innate potential for imagining the final separation from the world, or death. When a baby is born, it is vulnerable to pain and disintegration.

Robert Jay Lifton and Eric Olson, in *Living and Dying,* suggest that as a person passes through various stages of life, each new step, or "birth," brings with it new death anxieties that are associated with the inborn imagery of separation, existence, and disintegration. The responses of young children to separation from their mothers has already been mentioned in connection with children's fears. Again and again, one finds that when fear is present, a child or adult seeks comfort in the nearness of a familiar person or place.

As discussed in an earlier chapter, some children suffer from school phobia, which is not truancy or a fear of school, but is primarily anxiety about separating from home and mother. John Bowlby, in his book, *Attachment and Loss,* emphasized the importance of the mother or attachment figure in the development of a child's personality. Inadequate parenting can cause a disruption of the normal balance between attachment and independent, exploratory behavior, and can lead to a condition that Bowlby termed "anxious attachment." Fear of separation in childhood may play a significant part in the development of anxiety states in adult life. Some parents use the threat of abandonment or separation as a form of discipline, never intending to carry out such a threat. This kind of suggestion can provoke undue anxiety and feelings of insecurity in children.

Telling young children that only babies are afraid, or making fun of them, does not reduce fears. Reassurance and frank discussion of real dangers are helpful. Children can become less fearful if they are helped to become familiar with frightening situations a little at a time. Getting acquainted with a puppy or small dog may make a large dog seem less frightening. Parents and older brothers and sisters should realize that it is normal for children to have some fears. They should not be forced into overcoming their fears until they are ready. Throwing or dragging a young child into a swimming pool or lake may only hamper the process of learning to swim.

It has been shown that the presence or absence of a mother or other trusted person greatly influences the degree of fear to which a child responds. For instance, if a mother goes to the hospital for an emergency operation, a child may have nightmares, and small fears may become big ones. On the other hand, a situation that might be very frightening to a child alone (such as being lost in the woods) does not arouse much fear if a parent is present.

How one learns to cope with fears during early childhood may play a very important part in how one copes with fears in later life.

CHAPTER 5

Death and Dying

Fear of death is probably universal. Death has always been frightening and mysterious, even though it happens to each person. Freud stated that it was not possible to imagine one's own death, and that unconsciously, everyone believes he or she is really immortal. Certainly, most people find it difficult to conceive of the world going on without them, and most would rather push aside thoughts of dying. Judith Viorst, in her book *Necessary Losses*, recalls that, as a child, she knew that God could not take death away, but she asked him to arrange for her not to think about it.

Through the ages, people have tried to find ways of gaining immortality. The ancient Egyptians preserved the dead person's body and provided the tomb with all the material possessions and comforts he had in life, even including animals, slaves, and food; in this way, the individual was supposed to be able to live on. Even today, some people arrange to have their bodies frozen after death, in the hope that scientists will discover a way to restore them to life in the future. For many, the promise of an afterlife helps to ease the thought of dying. Another way of achieving a kind of immortality is through one's children, who carry on the biological continuity. Others circumvent death by creating great works of art or by performing great deeds that will be remembered after they are gone. One young man who was dying of leukemia wrote that he found comfort in the Eastern view of life as an endless cycle. Birth and death are not clear beginnings or endings, but events in an eternal process. Individuals may die, but the cycles of nature continue.

Psychiatrist Robert Jay Lifton says that the search for symbolic immortality, or a sense of continuity, is a part of being human. The awesome possibility of total annihilation in a nuclear holocaust severely threatens this expectation of the continuity of life in the future. But the fact remains that everyone someday must face the final separation from his or her own life on earth.

The word death is avoided, sometimes even at funerals, and the language used may omit direct references to death. Dead people are referred to as "loved ones" or "dearly departed" and are "laid to rest" rather than buried. They are shown at viewings with peaceful smiles. Careful cosmetic grooming makes them appear as lifelike as possible. Every effort is made to help the living conceal the fact of death from themselves as long as possible.

In modern industrialized societies, with the decline of mortality from treatable and preventable diseases or famine, natural death is much less common than it used to be, especially among the young. Death happens mainly to the elderly, and more likely than not, it happens in a hospital rather than at home. So death has become less familiar to the young and seems less a part of a normal cycle to everyone. In the nineteenth century, there was scarcely a person, young or old, who had not been to numerous funerals or who had not been present at the bedside of a dying relative. Mobs of curious people witnessed death at public executions, which were finally abolished toward the end of the nineteenth century.

English anthropologist Geoffrey Gorer has written about the "pornography of death," noting that, while sex was considered obscene in the prudish Victorian era, natural death has become obscene and pornographic in this century. Even though natural death has become taboo, there has been a greater emphasis on violent death. Western movies, spy stories and television programs, war stories, and horror novels and movies all are full of violence and killing. Gorer believes that we need to treat the subject of natural death as openly as we now deal with the subject of sex, instead of perpetrating the pornography.

The taboo about death that prevents many people from being comfortable with the subject has lifted somewhat in recent years, but widespread education is needed to help people attain a more open attitude toward dying. Not many years ago, medical schools avoided the topic of death. Many doctors and nurses working in hospitals concentrated on saving lives and evaded any meaningful dialogue with terminally ill patients about their concerns with death. Since the function of a hospital is to cure, death is considered a failure there.

Doctors are as fearful of death as are their patients. If they can learn to face openly their own fears and feelings of helplessness in the presence of death, they can come to grips with their apprehensions. Only if doctors, nurses, social workers, and others who work with terminally ill people are able to resolve their own fears can they lend psychological support to their dying patients.

Psychologist Robert J. Kastenbaum cites an experiment of his in which he asked women to interview a man they thought to be a hospital patient. Some of the women were merely told that the man was sick, while others were told that he was terminally ill. The first group reacted more warmly to the man than the group that thought he was dying. The latter seemed to shrink away and avoid eye contact. Professor Kastenbaum reported that even those women who had expressed an open attitude about death in a questionnaire seemed uncomfortable when confronted with a man they thought was dying.

Still, many signs of new attitudes about the frightening subject of death and dying have been evident during the past decade or two. In addition to improvement in many hospital situations, there is a new openness and curiosity about the subject among people in general. Many books about death and dying have been written. In addition to professional journals devoted to the subject, there are numerous articles on death in a wide variety of publications for the general reader as well as for professional healers, the clergy, and social workers. Courses and symposiums on death are popular at many age levels. No longer is fear of death a subject reserved for the very old.

Dr. Elisabeth Kübler-Ross, a Swiss psychiatrist practicing in the United States, has done much to alter attitudes about death and dying. Dr. Kübler-Ross reports that she seldom saw a dead person during her training as a hospital resident. The dead appeared to be almost magically whisked out of sight. Since that time, her work with physicians, nurses, and terminally ill patients has helped alleviate the fear of death for many. Her book, *Death and Dying,* is credited as a motivating force in encouraging more open dialogue about death and easing patients' concerns.

Kübler-Ross described five stages through which the terminally ill seem to pass. At first, there is shock and disbelief. Even though denial may not be total, the awful and fearful prospect of death is too much to accept immediately. Then there is a period of anger, which may be expressed against those who are able to live longer. This is followed by a period of bargaining with God or fate in the hope of gaining more time to do things yet undone. People plead with God for an extra week, or month, or year. This is followed by a stage of depression in which the dying person mourns his or her own death and the loss of loved ones and the things that are meaningful in life. Then there is an acceptance of the oncoming death, a quiet calm, and a willingness to live the remaining days as fully as possible.

Not everyone agrees with Dr. Kübler-Ross. Not all dying people go through each of these stages. Some do better if they cling to their denial, and others remain angry and bitter until the end. There is no "right" way to die. The important point is that dying people need to share their feelings and to get support, so that they do not feel isolated and rejected.

Sometimes, terminally ill people are subjected to heroic measures in an effort to save their lives, even if they are emotionally ready to die, and sometimes even if they are in a coma and brain dead. There has been much discussion and controversy about the ethics of "pulling the plug," that is, disconnecting life support systems when it is clear that the individual cannot recover and has no awareness of his or her surroundings. For many people, the quality of life is very important. They would rather be allowed to die with dignity than to suffer helplessly for a prolonged period of time. A dying person should be helped to achieve whatever is an appropriate death for him or her.

Although fear and anger about death remain with many individuals to the end of their lives, the care of the dying has been changing. Home care for the dying has improved, so terminally ill people can choose to die at home, surrounded by those who love them and in familiar surroundings, rather than in the impersonal atmosphere of a hospital room.

Growing numbers of the terminally ill are spending their last days in hospices, specially designed facilities for the dying, where they receive emotional support as well as nursing care and medication. The hospices are cheerful, homelike places where families and even pets may visit and stay. Although the first modern hospice was established in England in 1948, the tradition goes back to the Middle Ages, when hospices were set up in Europe to provide lodging for pilgrims who were traveling to and from religious sites. Hospices at that time were built also to shelter and care for the elderly, orphans, and the incurable. Modern hospices in the United States and abroad follow this medieval tradition of providing comfort and helping the dying to achieve an appropriate, dignified death.

Many adults try to shield children from death because they themselves are so uncomfortable with it. Since our culture teaches us to mask our own fear, anger, grief, and helplessness at the prospect of death, this is not surprising.

Communicating feelings and talking about fears can help children deal with death and relieve unrealistic anxieties or feelings of guilt when a loved one dies. Magical thinking is common among young children. A child may believe that something has happened because he thought about it. For instance, a little girl who was angry at her sister wished that she were an only child. When the sister was killed in an automobile accident a week later, the little girl felt very guilty because she thought she was the cause of her sister's death. In some cases, a child may think it is not safe to love because a person close to him or her has died. The child may think that others whom s/he loves may die and leave. He or she may develop increased fears about temporary separations. Open discussions with children can help avoid serious conflicts and difficulties.

When children are terminally ill, they often suffer more than necessary because of the way they are treated by adults. It has been found that parents, doctors, and nurses tend to lessen the amount of contact with a terminally ill child. The child may feel additional anxieties because of this increasing isolation. The adults do not purposely add to the child's problems, but their own fear of death prevents them from dealing comfortably and openly with problems of dying. Experts encourage parents to answer a child's questions about the seriousness of his or her illness honestly, while at the same time being reassuring.

In the view of some psychiatrists and psychologists, as noted earlier, birth itself, the first experience of separation, is the precursor for the development of later feelings about death. About the age of eighteen months, children begin to recognize the existence of death, but until the age of four or five, they do not recognize that it is final. Many young boys and girls help to bury pets, and then expect them to come alive again the next morning or next season. A young child cannnot understand that the separation is permanent when a parent or other loved one dies. He or she may think that death is a kind of sleep, or that the dead person has gone away temporarily.

Between the ages of five and nine, children begin to understand the finality of death. Many children in this age group think of death as a person or a kind of angel who carries people away. The grandfather of one five-year-old boy died just before a planned visit to the child's family. Upon being told of the death, the boy cried, "If he had only left New York a day sooner, he wouldn't be dead now."

By the age of nine or ten years, most children understand that death is inevitable and that it happens to everyone. These stages describe general patterns, but do not necessarily apply to all children. Feelings about death evolve and change during every stage of life, from birth to the moment of death.

Since the biological purpose of fear is to secure survival, fear of death is not unnatural. Fear is caused by the threat of separation and loss, and the loss of one's life is indeed total and final.

CHAPTER 6

Animal Fears

Fear reactions in cats, dogs, lions, gorillas, people, and other animals differ from species to species and from individual to individual. There is much overlap in the things that arouse fear in humans and those that arouse fear in other species, and certain situations appear generally to be feared more than others. Learning about the fears of various kinds of animals has helped individuals to understand and cope with their own fears and helped therapists in their work with people. It has even played a part in the way some veterinarians care for pets.

How can fear in animals be recognized? In addition to the obvious reactions of fight or flight, some responses are similar to the ones exhibited by frightened people. These include "freezing," curling up, taking cover, seeking the company of others, and calling for help. Many humans recognize the alarm calls of birds and mammals by their very tone. [Various species of birds and mammals use the alarm calls of another species as warnings to escape danger.] A wide variety of animals respond to potential danger cues through their senses of smell, sight, and/or hearing.

Fear responses to a sudden approach or strangeness are common. The fear of strangeness has an interesting aspect in the case of imprinting, which occurs with certain animals, especially birds that live on the ground and mammals that live in flocks. The term *imprinting* can be defined as the learning of parental characteristics by young animals. Imprinting takes place during a very brief period of time early in the life of the animal.

Pet geese are often the subject of experiments that show how animals learn to recognize the security of parents and to fear other animals. Professor Konrad Lorenz, a famous Viennese naturalist, used the eggs of the graylag goose in a popular experiment to demonstrate imprinting. After the eggs hatched, he discovered that the goslings would become attached to any large moving object, including himself, if they were separated from their mother during the imprinting period. They would follow Professor Lorenz in a long line across the fields, much as they would have followed their real mother.

Very young chicks will follow a person who clucks and walks away, and many other animals show this kind of socialization. Normally, the young become agitated and frightened when they are separated from the mother or mother object. This and other facts have led scientists to believe that imprinting reduces anxiety.

Pet dogs show signs of imprinting in the form of attachment to the dogs or people to whom they are exposed during the third to seventh week after birth. All new puppies who become pets experience socialization. Have you ever watched a puppy getting acquainted in its new home? If a puppy was born in a kennel and very few people touched it, talked to it, or spent time nearby for the fiirst five weeks of its life, the puppy may be afraid of the people who take it home even though they are kind to it. But after a few weeks of gentle handling, fear reactions disappear. If puppies are handled by people at three or four weeks of age, most dogs show no fear reactions by the time they are five weeks old.

Suppose a litter of puppies is allowed to run wild without any attention from people for a period of 12 weeks. Such puppies will be very timid when near humans and almost impossible to handle. They may need some hand-feeding and much loving care to overcome their fear of people. Keeping them in a confined area helps, but scientists who study animal behavior believe that dogs who have no contact with humans during the first 12 weeks of their lives will always be somewhat timid around human beings and will be less responsive as pets than those handled by people from birth.

Pets are frequently selected for the reputation of the breed's disposition. For example, basset hounds, spaniels, poodles, and dachshunds are known for their mild temperaments. Others may have characteristics that make them unsuitable for families with young children. But there are variations of fear responses even in dogs of the same breed.

Dogs and humans share many traits, and one of these is fear. Scientists at the Neuropsychiatric Laboratory of North Little Rock Veterans Administration Hospital in Arkansas began breeding two different strains of purebred pointers in an effort to study their behavior. They bred one line of pointers that developed abnormal behavior of a "neurotic" type and one line that was stable. Dr. Oddist D. Murphee and his colleagues explored the behavior of these different strains of pointers over a period of years, using a wide variety of tests. Nothing was done to aggravate or increase the timidity of the nervous strain of dogs. They were studied in relation to the stable strain to try to learn more about environmental and hereditary differences.

The behavior of the nervous strain was characterized by excessive timidity, extreme startle response, reduced activity in exploring surroundings, and marked avoidance of humans as well as frequent immobility in their presence. Some nervous dogs actually became rigid with fear in the presence of humans; if a person pushed the dog's head down, its back feet would actually spring up.

While dogs are not true models for human behavior disorders, there *are* many common characteristics. For example, some of the mind-body related, or psychosomatic, illnesses suffered by humans are also present in dogs. And the symptoms of rigid posture found in some emotionally disturbed people are also seen in some dogs.

Another approach to the study of fear in animals is demonstrated by the work of Dr. F. Brunner, a physician at the Veterinary Hospital in Vienna, Austria. Dr. Brunner worked with dogs and cats that had behavioral disorders that caused problems for their owners as well as for the pets themselves. He did not believe that there was enough knowledge to determine whether certain fears and other behavior problems were caused by the animal's environment or by heredity. Many individual behavior variations become serious problems, however. Treatment or therapy by a professional trainer can often change the situation and, in some cases, actually save the life of the pet.

Take the case of Chauncey, an overly fearful sheep dog who would jump on his master's bed during thunderstorms. The fright response first occurred at the age of three years after the dog was left alone in the house during a violent storm. Corrective training through a method known as conditioning helped Chauncey to overcome his abnormal fear of thunderstorms. The therapist-trainer could not explain to the dog that thunder was harmless, but noises similar to those made by thunder were simulated at the clinic and followed by the gentle, reassuring voice of the trainer. When the dog, who had jumped on the bed, became calm, the trainer led him off the bed with a leash and praised him for getting off the bed. After each thunderclap, the procedure was repeated. Petting him, praising him, and staying close to him helped reassure Chauncey that nothing would harm him when there was a loud noise. This procedure helped to reduce Chauncey's fear of thunder.

Field observers of monkeys and apes report similar fears in these animals. P. Jay, a scientist who studied the behavior of a type of monkey in India, reported that forest groups gradually became accustomed to her presence so that she could follow them at a distance of about 50 feet. But when the monkeys were startled by any sudden noise or movement in the brush, they immediately fled from sight.

Fleeing is one major kind of fear response; seeking physical contact with companions is another. Enthologist Jane van La-wick-Goodall carried out a long-term study of chimpanzees in Tanzania and included much information about fear responses in her detailed reports. One interesting observation concerned the hugging she witnessed between both young and old chimpanzees when they were frightened.

Many fears that people experience and many ways of handling these fears are better understood because of animal observation and experimentation. Fear of snakes is common among some birds, monkeys, apes, and humans; but whether this fear is learned or inborn is still a matter of dispute among experts. Certainly, fear of snakes is very intense in old world monkeys and apes.

When snakes were released in the monkey house of the London Zoo many years ago, the monkeys fled and screamed. But lemurs crowded to the front of the cages to watch the snakes. Lemurs are small, nocturnal animals that have large eyes, soft fur, and long tails. They belong to the family of primates which includes monkeys, apes, and man, and their natural habitat is Madagascar and adjacent islands. This area is one of the few parts of the world where there are no poisonous snakes. At first glance, the difference in fear response between the lemurs and the monkeys might appear to be proof that fear of snakes is inborn protection developed through evolution. But it also might be interpreted to be the result of the handing down of a learned fear from one generation to the next. Many animal behaviorists have shown that some wild species pass on a learned fear from one generation to the next. Humans are not alone in cultural traditions that teach survival techniques.

According to some theories, the fear of snakes may be due

to fear of certain types of movement. But wild chimpanzees have shown fear of snakes whether they were moving quickly or sleeping quietly. And chimpanzees who are raised in zoos do not always show fear when confronted with a snake.

While many humans are mildly squeamish in the presence of snakes, only 20 percent of the students who were tested in one study expressed intense fear of them. Of this group, only 1 to 2 percent actually avoided snakes when in their presence.

While fear is an inborn emotional response in higher animals, only certain situations seem to evoke fear on cue. For example, humans may be genetically biased to respond to writhing motions with fear, since these motions represent a clue to danger. In humans, the form and intensity of fears vary with maturation. Because most adults have learned so many new behaviors, traces of early fears are obscured; but these early fears may have an unconscious influence on the development of anxieties and phobias later in their lives, as mentioned earlier.

CHAPTER 7

Fears in a High-Tech Society

We live in a frightening world. Fearful news bombards us from all directions. Every day in the newspaper we read about the things people worry about, disasters that have occurred or are waiting to happen. On TV we hear about troublesome issues ranging from math phobia in young women to "high-tech" anxiety about risks of using modern technology.

Everyone was horrified to learn that on April 25, 1986, something went wrong in a nuclear reactor at Chernobyl, in the Soviet Union. The resulting fire and explosion killed some workers outright. Others were killed or seriously injured by high doses of radiation. Winds carried radioactive fallout across the Soviet Union and Europe, and even over the United States. Early news reports carried erroneous rumors that thousands in the U.S.S.R. had died and were being buried in mass graves. One hundred thousand people were evacuated from the 18-mile danger area surrounding the reactor. Of the thousands of children in this number, some appeared outwardly calm, but many were worried and depressed and expected to die. When several children were warned to stay out of the sun, so as not to add any ultraviolet radiation to the radiation they had already received, they became very sad because they thought they would never be allowed in the sun again. Many Americans feared that there was danger in the United States as well. One woman in California even bought a gas mask.

Relatively few people died outright in the Chernobyl explosion and in the weeks and months that followed, but no one knows how many will die years from now, since radiation causes both long- and short-term effects. It causes most damage to tissue whose cells reproduce rapidly, such as hair follicles, bone marrow, and intestinal tract. The higher the dose of radiation, (measured in units known as rem) the sooner and more severe are the effects. Doses of 1,000 rem or more are always fatal; this amount over the whole body would probably cause death in several days. Half of the people exposed to 400 rem over a period of a few days would recover, but the rest would die. Radiation sickness causes nausea, vomiting, diarrhea, and hair loss. By damaging the bone marrow, it stops the production of red and white blood cells and platelets. The results are severe anemia, bleeding, and decreased resistance to infection because of damage to the immune system. In some cases, bone marrow transplants have helped victims survive.

The long-term effects on the 100,000 people exposed to radiation in the Chernobyl accident cannot be predicted accurately. Scientists know that radioactive particles can be absorbed into human body tissues and may cause cancer many years after exposure.

"Can Chernobyl happen here?" asks a newsletter from the Union of Concerned Scientists. Many Americans are afraid that it could, and some think that radiation is the twentieth-century plague.

Even when nuclear power plants are operating safely, there is legitimate concern about radiation from the wastes that they produce. "Where can we bury 75,000 tons of nuclear waste already generated from power plants in the United States?" a magazine article queries. People worry that the storage sites may leak and contaminate groundwater. Others, in economically depressed areas, seem unconcerned about safety, and see the establishment of waste-disposal sites in their communities as a means of providing new jobs. For them, concern for financial security is stronger than concern about health.

Here is another relatively new fear about radiation in the environment: "Showers may pose cancer risk," states a headline in a newsletter of the American Medical Association. According to a spokesman from the Environmental Protection Agency (EPA), the water used by about a quarter of all homes in the United States contains radon, a radioactive gas emitted by decaying uranium particles. Exposure is higher in the New England area because of the natural presence of uranium in the soil and rock. Drinking the water is not so dangerous as breathing the water vapor. Inhaling radon particles into the lungs causes risk of cancer. Of the 120,000 lung cancer deaths per year, between 100 and 1,000 can be linked to radon in the water. According to one source, the radon level in water in some states carries a cancer risk equal to smoking one pack of cigarettes a day.

The EPA is in the process of developing standards for radon levels in water. There are kits for testing water for radon, and radon can be filtered out of water systems. Making sure that your home has proper ventilation, especially in winter, when many houses are sealed tightly, is another way of preventing the accumulation of radon. Even if the risk is overestimated, it is worrisome, all the more so because we cannot see, smell, or feel it.

Radiation can help as well as harm. Many people have been safely and successfully treated with radiation, but occasionally a freak accident occurs. Mr. Cox, a young oil field worker in Texas, was undergoing radiation therapy for a tumor on his shoulder. Because he had received eight previous treatments, he knew the procedure was short and painless. But on this occasion, when the technician turned on the machine, Mr. Cox saw a flash of light, heard a sizzling sound, and felt a pain in his shoulder like an electric shock. He was then hit by another burst in the neck, and he jumped off the table, calling for help. The technician outside the room neither saw the accident nor heard the patient call, because the video monitor was not plugged in, and the intercom was not working. Another man died three weeks after an over-dose of radiation from the same machine. Doctors and technicians worked for a long time to unravel the mystery of what went wrong with this extremely complicated computerized linear accelerator radiation machine. Accidents such as these are very rare, but people remember them rather than the hundreds of safe and successful treatments.

High technology can be frightening in other ways. Many fear that its use may eventually result in disaster if the possible consequences are not considered with great care. For example, Kurt Gottfried, a Cornell University physicist, questions the trustworthiness of the proposed "star-wars" shield. He likens the shield to a flotilla of orbiting nuclear plants whose performance under attack would be unknown. Such a situation is scary to imagine, despite assurances that this shield would provide a good defense and reduce the chance of nuclear destruction.

In his book, *The Broken Connection,* psychiatrist Robert Jay Lifton discusses a condition that he terms "nuclearism," a kind of secular religion based on technology. He believes that the ardent commitment of many persons to the policy of developing more and deadlier nuclear weapons is the result of anxiety about nuclear destruction. Allying themselves with the power of nuclear force makes them feel safer. They feel that nuclear weapons are absolutely necessary in order to prevent destruction. Lifton thinks that everyone has terrible anxieties about the possibility of total annihilation, but that some people tend to distance them-selves and avoid facing such a prospect. The result is, in Lifton's words, a pervasive "nuclear numbing." This can be a dangerous attitude, because it blinds us to the existence of real threats. Lifton believes that anxiety can serve a good purpose in decision-making about the use of nuclear power. Confronting the anxiety and heeding the danger signals may indeed save us from destruction.

People are often lulled into a false sense of security. For instance, after many successful launches into space, space travel was beginning to seem almost as risk-free as plane travel. Then the shuttle Challenger blew up in January 1986, killing all seven astronauts aboard, including teacher Christa McAuliffe, as millions of horrified spectators watched on television. Defective sealer rings in the solid-fuel boosters were later found to be the cause of the disaster. A marvel of technology had gone awry, and the accident shocked many Americans out of their complacent attitude.

High-tech risks are involved when we entrust ourselves to complicated technology in combination with the chance of human error. No wonder that some people call this the age of fear.

Another modern fear is the fear of AIDS, acquired immune-deficiency syndrome. One woman wanted to know if she could contract AIDS from a book that was handled by a gay librarian. Parents and children picketed schools, carrying signs with slogans such as "Keep AIDS out of public schools." This deadly disease is certainly a new cause for fear. The first well-documented cases occured in 1981, and the disease did not have a name until 1982. As of June 1, 1987, about 37,000 cases of AIDS had been reported in the United States, and over 20,000 of these had resulted in death. It has been predicted that 54,000 will die of AIDS in 1991.

Despite its seriousness, AIDS is, fortunately, not so contagious as many other diseases, and there is no evidence that it can be spread by casual contact. Yet a poll taken in 1985 indicated that half the people questioned thought that AIDS could be transmitted by casual contact. Many people have succumbed to irrational thinking and behavior, a "plague mentality" based on ignorance, reminiscent of the climate of fear during the Black Plague in the fourteenth century. Perhaps AIDS is the twentieth-century plague, not because scientists still have no cure, but because of the public's fear and lack of knowledge about the disease. The Surgeon General of the United States recently issued a report recommending a vigorous campaign against AIDS. A widespread drive to educate people and dispel myths can relieve many of the uncertainties and fears about this disease.

Another new fear is the fear of terrorism. While the use of terrorist tactics as a political tool is not new, it has increased lately. Ten years ago, there were about ten terrorist acts a week worldwide; in 1986, about ten a day was the average. Bob's family was planning a trip to Europe, but then they began reading articles about the dangers of traveling. One travel magazine devoted a column to the "Do's and Don'ts" of avoiding terrorism abroad. (When flying, don't sit in the aisle; aisle passengers get hurt first.) It was not surprising that Bob and his family, like many other Americans, decided to cancel their plans to travel abroad in the summer of 1986. Terrorism is often directed against innocent targets, and terrorists can strike anyone, anywhere.

Becoming the victim of terrorists is a very traumatic experience. Most people in this situation follow a similar pattern of reactions. At first, they are shocked and numb and cannot believe the events that are occurring. Then, as the reality penetrates, intense fear arises. Most people in terrifying situations do not scream, run, or strike out heroically. In hostage situations, they are more likely to respond with a kind of paralysis, a state that one expert calls "frozen fright." In this state, a person may behave in a submissive, compliant manner, because he or she is so powerless. Sometimes, a strange bond forms between the captors and their hostages, occuring when victims and hostages remain in close contact with each other over a period of time.

This is called the Stockholm Syndrome, named after an incident that took place in Sweden in 1973. Psychiatrists and other experts believe that the syndrome is an unconscious response to the sudden traumatic experience of becoming a victim. The severe terror induces a state comparable to the helplessness of an infant. In this condition, the victim places his trust in the powerful captor, perceiving him as good, because the captor is allowing him to live. This psychological reaction helps the individual cope with the extreme stress he is experiencing. Former hostages often experience symptoms for weeks or months after they are rescued. They may suffer from depression, nightmares, flashbacks of the traumatic events, anxiety attacks, and phobias. In one instance of a train hijacking, one third of the surviving victims later developed train phobias.

The odds against being held hostage by terrorists are high. Some people overreact and worry unnecessarily, but the possibility is nonetheless real.

While no one denies the seriousness of potential dangers in today's world, we need not be trapped in a prison of fear. Even though we cannot always control external events, we can combat their effect on our life.

CHAPTER 8

Horror

If everyone is really so worried about what might happen, why are horror movies and stories so popular? People are both repelled and fascinated by nearly everything gruesome and gory. They stop on the highway to stare at the scene of an accident, exclaiming at the destruction. Recently, it was reported in the newspaper that a number of onlookers waited patiently for three hours while the rescue squad pried someone out of a wrecked car with the device known as the "jaws of life." In this case, the driver was dead, but the spectators wanted a glimpse of the mangled body. Accidents, disasters, suicides, and murders are all powerfully fascinating subjects.

In October 1986, a gruesome horror novel called *It* jumped to the top of the best-seller list immediately upon publication. The most popular films and videotape rentals had such titles as *I Dismember Mama, Aliens, Friday the Thirteenth,* and *The Fly.* The latter is a story about a man whose molecules become mixed with those of a housefly, and the film depicts his revolting transformation. "Sweeney Todd" was a widely acclaimed musical play based on the true story of the "demon barber of Fleet Street." Todd, who lived in London in the nineteenth century, slashed his customers' throats, then ground up their bodies and made meat pies of them.

Scary rides in amusement parks, haunted houses, and

59

spooky graveyards are fun because they give people the opportunity to prove to themselves that they will not really be hurt by
these experiences. When we go through a haunted house in an
amusement park, we expect something scary to happen. The
hallway is dark, and spider webs are hanging all around. Of
course, we know they are not real and that whatever makes us
jump will not really hurt us. Still, we enjoy the fun of feeling
frightened while knowing there is no real harm.

Superstition is often a "fun" fear. Playing games with fear is
common and serves a special purpose. The masks at Halloween
are more for fun than fear, but there is an element of fear
involved. Halloween is the eve of All Hallows, or All Saints' Day,
and, in some faiths, is devoted to the dead who are blessed and
in heaven. It was a day of devotion to the memory of the dead
even in pre-Christian times, but in America today, much of the
original meaning has been forgotten. Symbols of death, such as
skeletons, skulls, cross-bones, witches, devils, and ghosts are still
part of the holiday scene. Today one might consider the child-
ghosts as ancestral souls returning from the dead to frighten the
adults who have neglected their memory. Child-ghosts are ap-
peased with candy and small change, tokens of sacrifices once
offered on the graves of the dead. Ancient burial rituals sometimes included a small payment for fare over the Styx, the river
across which the souls of the dead were ferried to the under-
world. Dr. Martin Grotjahn, in *Beyond Laughter,* suggests that
the pumpkin head with lighted candle may represent the funeral
bier with the head of the slain enemy as a trophy. He also points
out that parents symbolically repeat the ancient sacrifice of
children by allowing them to represent the dead in their Halloween costumes, although this meaning remains in the unconscious.

Scary and gruesome stories have always held a fascination
for people, dating back to ancient times. The Greek myths

abound with creatures such as Medusa, with her hair of live serpents, who turned her victims to stone if they looked at her. Almost everyone remembers enjoying the horrors of fairy tales, with their wicked stepmothers, witches, and monsters. Bruno Bettelheim describes the use of fear in fairy tales in his book, *The Uses of Enchantment*. This famous psychologist describes the child's unconscious as a battleground full of terrifying fears, death wishes, and hatreds. The violence in fairy tales helps to allay the child's fears by showing that s/he is not the only one who imagines such awful happenings. While fairy tales may frighten a child for a short period of time, Dr. Bettelheim observes that their happy endings dispel anxiety. Who cannot imagine himself lost in the woods, as Hansel and Gretel were? This is not an uncommon occurence. But then suppose a wicked witch grabbed you and locked you in a cage, with the intention of cooking and eating you. Many adults can recall the wonderful mixture of fear and delight they felt upon hearing that story, even after numerous retellings.

One of the most prolific and successful horror writers is Stephen King, the author of *It*. He thinks that reading and experiencing fears vicariously are good ways for people to exorcise the darker side of their feelings. New York psychiatrist Dr. Robert Gould explains that horror is "extremely distracting." It takes our minds away from the fears of the real world into a fantasy world that we can control, and this is the reason for its popularity.

Some Indiana University psychologists, in a study of college students, found that women whose male companions exhibited no signs of fear during horror movies rated the men more attractive. The men, on the other hand, were more attracted to women who showed fear. The researchers suggested that watching scary movies is a vicarious way for men to feel macho. It is a good feeling to conquer one's fear, even if you do it vicariously.

Not everyone can be an automobile racer, test pilot, or mountain climber.

Horror in movies, on television, or in stories brings the observer or reader to the scene in such a way that s/he is a participant in a dangerous act while in a safe place.

CHAPTER 9

Dealing with Stress

Do you worry about some of the problems mentioned in Chapter 7, and do you wonder about how others deal with their fears? The way people feel is often related to how much control they think they have over their lives.

Shortly after the Challenger spaceship exploded, thirteen-year-old Jon came home from school and asked his mother, "What does NASA stand for?" Jon answered his own question: "Need Another Seven Astronauts."

Other "sick jokes" were making the rounds.

The children were shocked by the tragedy and trying to find an outlet for their feelings.

Jon had been shocked and distressed when he watched the liftoff of Challenger on television. He could hardly believe what he was seeing as the ship exploded. Surely nothing could have gone wrong, he thought; space flight has become so routine and safe that ordinary people like schoolteachers can ride into space. It is almost like taking a plane from New York to San Francisco.

Jon began to think that nothing was as safe and secure as he had always assumed. He felt prickles of anxiety when he thought about all the bad things that could happen.

Why did Jon tell those awful jokes? Were they a sign of sickness or degeneracy? No, say the experts. Jon was genuinely upset by the disaster and meant no disrespect for the dead astronauts. Children and adolescents, like adults, need to deal with their feelings about loss, death, and other threatening or stressful events. People tell bad jokes and use macabre humor in an attempt to master their feelings. Experts emphasize the point that it is very important for children and adults to express and share their feelings. According to Dr. Edward Kessler, a psychiatrist at Georgetown University, one reason for the profound impact of the spaceship deaths on younger children was that it disrupted their belief that adults can always make everything safe.

When some Canadian researchers surveyed a thousand junior high and high school students about their hopes and fears, nuclear war was the concern mentioned most often. Those who had more fear of nuclear war also had more concerns about their career plans and unemployment. The students who voiced less anxiety about their future and about nuclear war were more likely to think they did not have any influence. Those students who were more anxious about nuclear war tended to feel that they had some influence over the threat.

The researchers concluded that people who feel they have the power to help solve social problems can also tolerate the anxiety of thinking about these problems. The students who expressed little anxiety also expressed feelings of helplessness in regard to their impact on the future; they may have been defending themselves against their anxiety by denying the threat. The authors noted that people who acknowledge and face their fears are more likely to take action.

Many people are beset by worries, fears, and stress in their lives. Studies in animals and humans have shown that stress can affect the nervous system, the heart, the immune system, metabolism, and hormone levels.

Can you die of fright?

Take the case of Mrs. King, a sixty-year-old woman who owned a small grocery store. One night, when she happened to be working there alone, a young man with a gun burst into the store and demanded money of the terrified woman. After taking the contents of the cash register, he ran off, and she called the police. While she was talking with them, she began having palpitations and trouble breathing. Two hours later, she died in a hospital. She had no history of previous heart problems, but, according to the medical report, a severe disruption of normal heart rhythm, or arrhythmia, was the cause of death. Mrs. King literally died of fright.

Other such cases have been described. In 1856, a deaf-mute girl died while being chastised publicly. Two of her siblings had also died suddenly under stressful circumstances. One researcher found that 20 percent of persons who have had life-threatening arrhythmias or who died of cardiac arrest had undergone severe psychological stress within the previous 24 hours.

Some experts think that this kind of sudden death may be caused by a surge of sympathetic nervous system activity and release of certain chemicals that disrupt the normal electrical activity of the heart. One study showed that people with panic disorder had changes in their heart rhythm during panic attacks. The subjects wore monitoring devices that recorded cardiac activity while they carried out their normal daily routines. All experienced panic attacks at some point, and these attacks occurred at the same times at which the abnormal heart rhythms were recorded. Some people are "hot reactors," whose bodies and minds may be overly sensitive even to minimally stressful events. Other people stay cool under very trying circumstances.

When people are continually subjected to the fight-or-flight situation because of ongoing stress in their lives, eventually their bodies may be affected. It has been found that recently bereaved widowers have a sudden death rate 40 percent higher than married men of the same age. There is also evidence that distressed persons are more susceptible to infectious diseases and cancer. Studies done on a group of healthy medical students showed that, during final examinations, there was a significant decline in the level of natural killer cells in their blood. These cells are important in defending the body against cancer and some viruses.

Other factors such as job frustration, social isolation, depression, and rage can produce both immediate and long-term effects on a person's health. For example, in the 1960's, young engineers at the Kennedy Space Center had a 50 percent higher incidence of cardiovascular disease than was usual for men in that age group. One reason suggested was that the work force was being cut drastically, and these engineers responded to anxiety about their jobs with an increase in heart disease. Some researchers have observed that high-pressure, repetitive jobs, in which the individual has no control, are the most stressful. Contrary to what many people think, highly educated overachievers are not the most prone to heart attacks. Those who are unhappy and frustrated, or who are impatient and try to accomplish too much in too short a time are the people at risk.

Orchestra conductors, top executives, and persons in Who's Who all are among those who live longer. The emotionally healthy have goals in their lives, they feel in control, and they tend to enjoy challenges that might make other people anxious.

While there is no way of eliminating stress completely from the environment, there are ways of learning to deal with it and to keep the mind and body healthy. Some sources of stress can be avoided. For instance, trying to fit too many activities into a crowded schedule can make one feel pressured all day. If a person is realistic about what he or she can accomplish, and limits activities, that person is not always worrying about the unfinished things.

Finding time just to relax and do something enjoyable, even for a short time during the day, can relieve tension. Another good way of reducing anxiety is regular exercise. Having friendships and being able to talk about problems also can reduce feelings of tension. Meditation, the use of biofeedback, and even hypnosis are other techniques that can help to lessen the stress in life.

CHAPTER 10

Overcoming Anxieties

Everyone faces a variety of fears—external threats from the environment, as well as anxieties from within. Have you experienced some of the feelings and fears that have been described in this book? Perhaps you are not sure whether your anxieties are normal or excessive. You may be interested in checking yourself by filling out the following inventory devised by Dr. David Burns. Put a check in the column that best corresponds to the amount of worry that item has caused you during the past week. Of course, the purpose of the test is to provide a rough estimate of the amount of anxiety, not to unearth the cause or to make a diagnosis.

A high score means that you are probably having more serious anxiety than most people. As noted earlier, anxiety can be a symptom of a number of conditions—physical illnesses, various emotional problems, drugs, alcohol, and even too much caffeine. If you are concerned that worries and anxieties are ruling your life and causing you distress, you can get help by seeking out a qualified professional. Your family doctor can probably refer you to a therapist. You can also call the mental health clinic in your town or city, or your local hospital for information about finding counselors.

Therapy can usually help an individual who has "normal" kinds of anxieties or who suffers from generalized anxiety. By

Burns Anxiety Inventory

	Not at all 0	Somewhat 1	Moderately 2	A lot 3

Category I: Anxious Feelings

1. Anxiety, nervousness, worry or fear
2. Feeling that things around you are strange, unreal or foggy
3. Feeling detached from all or part of your body
4. Sudden, unexpected panic spells
5. Apprehension or a sense of impending doom
6. Feeling tense, stressed, "uptight" or on edge

Category II: Anxious Thoughts

7. Difficulty concentrating
8. Racing thoughts or having your mind jump from one thing to the next
9. Frightening fantasies or daydreams
10. Feeling that you're on the verge of losing control
11. Fears of cracking up or going crazy
12. Fears of fainting or passing out
13. Fears of physical illnesses or heart attacks or dying
14. Concerns about looking foolish or inadequate in front of others
15. Fears of being alone, isolated or abandoned
16. Fears of criticism or disapproval
17. Fears that something terrible is about to happen

Category III: Physical Symptoms

18. Skipping or racing or pounding of the heart (sometimes called palpitations)
19. Pain, pressure or tightness in the chest
20. Tingling or numbness in the toes or fingers
21. Butterflies or discomfort in the stomach
22. Constipation or diarrhea
23. Restlessness or jumpiness
24. Tight, tense muscles
25. Sweating not brought on by heat
26. A lump in the throat
27. Trembling or shaking
28. Rubbery or "jelly" legs
29. Feeling dizzy, light-headed or off balance
30. Choking or smothering sensations or difficulty breathing
31. Headaches or pains in the neck or back
32. Hot flashes or cold chills
33. Feeling tired, weak or easily exhausted

Total _____

Interpreting your anxiety score:

0–9: none or minimal; 10–19: mild; 20–29: moderate; 30–49: severe; 50–99: extreme or panic exploring past experiences and by looking at how a person deals with the stress, the therapist can help him to identify problems, resolve conflicts, and handle stress in better ways. A therapist can also provide emotional support and aid in becoming more self-confident. Learning relaxation techniques and getting plenty of rest, good nutrition, and regular exercise can also help to decrease anxiety.

Sometimes tranquilizers like Valium or related compounds may be used for a few weeks at the outset of therapy, if anxiety is severe. Most psychiatrists recommend only short-term treatment with these drugs, because after about six weeks, there is generally little further improvement, and because there is the possibility of dependence or abuse. Needless to say, it can be very dangerous to use any such drugs without the supervision of a physician.

Traditional psychotherapy or other "talking cures" alone have not been found to be very successful in treating panic disorders or eliminating specific phobias. Most experts agree that the best treatment for simple phobias is exposure to the feared object or situation. The difficulty lies in persuading the fearful person to face whatever makes him anxious.

Phobia Free, Don't Panic, Stop Running Scared, Kicking the Fear Habit, and *Five-Minute Phobia Cure* are a few of the many books that deal with the subject of fear. While a person may not be able to get rid of a phobia in five minutes, almost everyone can be helped to overcome fears. The method used is called behavior therapy. Psychologists may employ any one of several different techniques, all of which have the goal of making the person face and conquer his fear instead of avoiding it.

The first person to use this technique was the psychologist Mary Cover Jones. In 1924, shortly after Watson had successfully induced fear in little Albert, she attempted to cure him and other fearful children by "deconditioning." She found that simply telling nice stories about friendly animals did not work. One child was afraid of small animals and other furry things. Jones introduced him into a group of children who had no fear of rabbits, and a rabbit was brought into the room during part of each session. When the fearful child saw the other children playing with the rabbit, he gradually lost his fears. Cover also offered candy to the children in combination with exposure to the rabbit. This method of combining a pleasurable experience with the feared object also seemed successful.

Exposure treatment was not widely used until after 1958, when Dr. Joseph Wolpe, a South African psychiatrist, introduced the approach known as systematic desensitization. Positive reinforcement such as praise for the patient's ability to relax after the feared object or a picture of it is presented helps. In Wolpe's technique, the sequence of events follows the pattern of *relax— imagine—relax—stop imagining.* For example, a person who has a phobia about hospitals but must undergo an operation might be instructed to imagine a picture of the outside of a hospital, then asked to stop picturing the hospital and go on relaxing. After a short time the person might next be told to picture the inside of a hospital, then asked to imagine him or herself in a hospital bed, and finally, after a series of steps, be guided to the operating table by the therapist. The first stimulus is the feared object or situation presented verbally in a mild form. The person continues to imagine increasingly fearful situations under the guidance of the therapist so that with each step some of the anxiety is dissipated. Eventually, the person can imagine the most fearful situation without the usual anxiety. When this happens, making the transition to facing the real object is accomplished with much less fear. This kind of exposure treatment is known as imaginal, because the exposure is in the person's imagination.

Implosion therapy is another variation of the imaginal technique. In this approach, the exposure is not gradual. Instead, the most anxiety-provoking situation is presented immediately. For instance, someone with a phobia about dogs may be asked to imagine a large, ferocious dog snarling and showing his fangs, then jumping a fence and chasing the person down the street.

In vivo exposure, or exposure in real life to the feared object, is a method that some psychologists and psychiatrists believe to be more effective than the imaginal techniques. Since the goal of all methods is facing the fear in real life, they reason that it is more efficient to begin by actual exposure. Various combinations of therapies have been used with success.

For example, consider the case of Tony. Tony was so afraid of water that he wore a life preserver when he took a bath. He was embarrassed to let his family know this and pretended he played a game with the preserver when in the tub. Tony knew it was silly to feel that he could drown in the tub, but he continued to live with his phobia until he heard about another boy at school who was being treated for a fear of closed places. Then he told his parents the truth about his life preserver. They were aware that Tony would never go in the water at the lake, nor would he go in a boat or participate in any other activities near water. But they had not realized the extent of his fear.

Part of Tony's treatment was to imagine that he was taking a bath in a very deep tub of water. Each small detail was described, and Tony was told to imagine that he was slipping under the water. "You are slipping lower and lower into the tub," suggested the psychologist. "Now the water is coming in your mouth and your nose." The first time Tony imagined this situation he was terribly frightened. But the scene was repeated again and again until he learned that the only terrible part of the experience was his own fear. Each time, he was made to imagine the worst thing that could happen; but although he even imagined drowning in the tub, he was never harmed.

During the sessions, the psychologist talked with Tony and discovered the origin of his intense fear through long periods of questioning. From time to time, he learned bits of information about Tony's early experiences and about one traumatic experience in which he had wandered off alone and nearly drowned in a shallow stream. Tony recalled that his mother had warned him many times not to go near the stream when he was alone because he might drown. Tony's phobia had existed for so long that he had forgotten about his terrible experience in the stream until he talked with the psychologist. He unlearned his fear of water by first imagining the most threatening situation, such as being immersed in deep water, then gradually becoming accustomed to actually bathing in shallow streams under pleasant and secure conditions.

Some therapists regularly use a "buddy" system. A friend of the phobic person is enlisted to accompany and encourage the person to follow through with the task of facing the feared situation. Sometimes, group situations can help. "Fearful Flyers" is one such program that has been successful in helping people overcome their fear of plane travel. Over a period of several weeks, the group is exposed to films, encouraging lectures, talks by others who have been helped, relaxation exercises, visits to the airport, and finally, a plane flight. Not everyone learns to love flying, but most people find that after these sessions, they are able to take plane trips without excessive anxiety. When the actor Sam Shepard was given the role of Chuck Yeager (the test pilot who was first to break the sound barrier) in the movie *The Right Stuff*, he was afraid to fly. Yaeger thought that the actor should know how it feels to fly, so Shepard was forced to go up in a jet. He, like others, got rid of his fear by facing it.

Parents can help young children overcome their fears by techniques similar to those used by Mary Cover Jones. For example, Susan had a school phobia. Her therapist taught her how to relax while she was imagining herself leaving her house— at first going only to the corner, then progressing until she imagined herself in the classroom. In the meantime, her parents helped her to practice short separations from them, such as walking around the corner and staying out of sight of her house for one minute at a time. The amount of time was gradually increased. Susan also received reward points for her successes. She began going to school accompanied by her mother, and eventually she was able to go on her own without becoming fearful about leaving home.

Some therapists use hypnosis as an aid in treating phobias. One therapist used it to help a patient relax so that she could make herself board a plane. She was able to think of the plane as an extension of her body and to imagine she was floating with it. She had no trouble flying subsequently. Another patient was phobic about washing her hair and was terrified when she had to do so. Under hypnosis, she was asked to explain her fear, and she described a scene from childhood in which her psychotic mother pushed her head under water while shampooing her hair. The patient was then able to deal with this phobia and overcome it.

Some people do not need therapists to cure them. Beverly was an avid skier, but she always felt nervous about riding the chairlift or the gondola. Swaying so far above the ground and looking down made her sick and dizzy. One summer, she toured the United States with two friends. They visited the Grand Canyon, and in order to see its spectacular beauty, they joined a group of people who were riding mules down to the Colorado River at the bottom. The trail was narrow and steep, blasted out of the sheer rock walls of the canyon, and there were no guard rails. This was an acrophobic's nightmare. But Beverly was determined not to miss this opportunity. Besides, her friends did not seem worried about entrusting their lives to the mules. So she went along, feeling scared and clinging tightly to the mule. At some places, she even closed her eyes because the heights were so terrifying.

As the hours went by, Beverly began to relax just a bit and started to pay more attention to the scenery than to her dry mouth and pounding heart. She survived the experience and felt proud. The following winter, on her first day of skiing, she noticed an interesting change. She realized that she was no longer afraid of riding the chairlift. The mule trip had cured her of her fear of heights.

Some people use alcohol or tranquilizers to deaden their fears, but these are not effective, even though they may temporarily decrease anxiety. The only effective treatment is to allow yourself to experience the anxiety and prove to yourself that it will not kill you or drive you crazy.

How it is possible to treat a panic attack by exposure therapy, when a panic attack, by definition, is spontaneous and not caused by a specific fear? Considering that panic disorder has a biological basis, it is not surprising that medications can help. Certain medications that have been used to combat depression have also been found to be very effective in preventing panic. The drugs most often used are imipramine and phenelzine. Although there is disagreement among researchers, some studies have demonstrated that Xanax, (a drug related to Valium in chemical structure), and other drugs in this family can also prevent panic.

Studies show that imipramine does not have any effect on simple phobias, but it does block the anxiety of school phobia in children. It also blocks the anticipatory anxiety in agoraphobics. Imipramine has also been given to panic-prone individuals in the laboratory experiments with intravenous sodium lactate described earlier. The imipramine was found to reduce the level of anxiety caused by the lactate. The fact that imipramine is effective against one kind of anxiety and not another tends to confirm the theory that simple phobias and panic attacks have different causes.

Many people who have panic attacks also suffer from agoraphobia and often have many other social phobias, such as fear of eating in public. Investigators have discovered that the best treatment for these people is a combination of medication and exposure. The drug dampens the overactivity of the nervous system and allows the person to face the anxiety-provoking situation and overcome his phobias.

Even someone who has severely restricted his life because of panic attacks and anxieties can be helped, if the disorder is recognized and diagnosed properly. Unfortunately, many people with panic attacks suffer needlessly because they have been dismissed as hypochondriacs and neurotics. With appropriate medication, behavior therapy, and supportive psychotherapy, along with encouragement from family and friends, these individuals can be helped to lead a fuller life.

Even though you may have many fears to face, from within yourself and from the world outside, taking positive action may help you feel less anxious. In spite of horrors, frights, and panic, you are relatively safe, and you can be in control of your life.

Glossary

Anxiety A state of apprehension, uneasiness, or tension, stemming from feelings of impending danger, either internal or external. Usually distinguished from fear in that there is no readily recognizable source of danger. Anxiety may be a symptom of numerous emotional disorders as well as physical disorders.

Behavior Therapy or Behavior Modification Treatment for changing behavior by manipulation of factors in the environment that are related to the behavior. Examples of this technique are conditioning and desensitization.

Conditioning Evocation of a response by a stimulus that does not normally provoke that response. This is done by pairing the neutral stimulus with the stimulus that prompts the response. An example is Watson's experiment with little Albert. The neutral stimulus (a white rat) was paired with a stimulus (a loud noise) that normally evoked fear in Albert. This process of conditioning produced fear in Albert in response to the white rat, even when the rat was presented without the noise.

Desensitization Therapy Treatment for phobias, based on exposure to the feared situation or object, employing various techniques, including imagined and *in vivo* (real life) exposure. Exposure may be graded, beginning with the least stressful experience and progressing, or it may begin with the most stressful situation.

Fear   Emotional and physical response to danger; reaction to a recognized threat that is characterized by an impulse to escape the danger and by feelings of disagreeable tension; "fight or flight" response.

Generalized Anxiety Disorder (GAD)   Generalized and persistent feelings of anxiety, lasting over a period of weeks or months, without the symptoms of phobic disorder or specific episodes of panic. Symptoms may include worrying, anticipation of misfortune, difficulties in concentrating, feeling jittery or irritable, eyelid twitching, muscle aches and tension, inability to relax, sweating, cold hands, high pulse rate, dry mouth, diarrhea or upset stomach, lightheadedness, and tingling of hands and feet.

Neurotransmitters   Chemicals in the nervous system that are involved in the transmission of impulses between neurons or nerve cells.

Panic Disorder   Recurrent, unpredictable, spontaneously occurring anxiety attacks characterized by intense feelings of apprehension, terror, or impending doom. Symptoms include some or all of the following: difficulty breathing, choking sensations, palpitations, chest pain, dizziness, faintness, tingling in hands or feet, shakiness, hot or cold flashes, feelings of unreality, fear of going crazy or losing control. Attacks usually are short-lived, lasting for about 5 to 20 minutes.

Phobic Disorders

Simple phobia   Irrational and persistent fear of a specific object, situation, or activity recognized by the individual as excessive, which also interferes with the person's life or functioning.

Social phobia Irrational apprehension and fear of embarrassment concerning situations in which the individual is exposed to scrutiny by others, such as eating or writing in public, using public bathrooms, or speaking in front of an audience.

Agoraphobia Fear of being in public places such as crowded streets, stores, or public transportation. Usually results in increasing constriction of the individual's life and activities. Often develops in association with panic attacks.

School Phobia Anxiety in children, related to leaving home to attend school. Not actually a fear of school, but rather a fear of separating from home and parents. Sometimes school phobia in childhood precedes development of panic disorder in adulthood.

Separation Anxiety Fear of separation from mother or other significant person.

Suggestions for Further Reading

Agras, W. Stewart. *Panic: Facing Fears, Phobias, and Anxiety.* New York: W. H. Freeman and Company, 1985.

Bower, S. A., and G. H. Bower. *Asserting Yourself: A Practical Guide for Positive Change.* New York: Addison-Wesley, 1976.

Cohen, Daniel and Susan. *Teenage Stress.* New York: M. Evans and Company, Inc., 1984.

Marks, I. M. *Living with Fear.* New York: McGraw-Hill, 1978.

Ornstein, R., and R. F. Thompson. *The Amazing Brain.* Boston: Houghton Mifflin, 1984.

Sheehan, David V. *The Anxiety Disease.* New York: Charles Scribner's Sons, 1983.

Silverstein, Herma. *Scream Machines: Roller Coasters Past, Present, and Future.* New York: Walker and Company, 1986.

Sutherland, E. Ann, Zalman Amit, and Andrew Weiner. *Phobia Free: How to Fight Your Fears.* New York: Stein and Day, 1977.

Viorst, Judith. *Necessary Losses.* New York: Simon and Schuster, 1986.

Wender, P. H., and Klein, D. F. *Mind, Mood, and Medicine.* New York: Farrar, Straus, Giroux, 1981.

Wolpe, J. *The Practice of Behaviour Therapy.* New York: Pergamon Press, 1969.

Index

About the Authors

Margaret O. Hyde is the author of more than fifty books for young people on topics that touch their lives. She has also written several documentaries for NBC-TV. In addition to writing and teaching, Hyde has served as science consultant for Lincoln School of Teachers College, Columbia University. A resident of Shelburne, Vermont, she lectures widely and has appeared on radio and television.

Elizabeth Forsyth, a psychiatrist, has collaborated with Margaret Hyde on four other books for young adults. A graduate of Yale University School of Medicine, she has served as clinical instructor in psychiatry at the University of Vermont College of Medicine, has been psychiatric consultant for the Burlington, Vermont, public school system, and currently combines private practice with forensic psychiatry.

Among the significant titles on which Hyde and Forsyth have collaborated are: *Know Your Feelings, What Have You Been Eating? Suicide: The Hidden Epidemic,* and *Terrorism: A Special Kind of Violence.*